Today I Am an American

by Fabiola Muñoz
illustrated by Frank Sofo

Orlando Boston Dallas Chicago San Diego

Visit *The Learning Site!*
www.harcourtschool.com

Those of us who were born in the United States are citizens of this country. Nothing more is required for us to remain citizens. We are not obliged to take any tests. We are not obliged to fill out any forms.

What about our parents or our grandparents? What about our neighbors or our friends? Many of them were not born here. They came to the United States from other countries. At some point, they were allowed to apply for United States citizenship. They became petitioners.

Petitioners for citizenship must learn about United States history and government. They must also learn about the rights and duties of being a United States citizen. Among the most important of these responsibilities are voting in elections and obeying our country's laws.

Before people can be granted a certificate of United States citizenship, they must do several things. They must have lived in the United States for at least five years. They need to fill out an application. They need to be interviewed by an examiner. The examiner asks them questions and helps them fill out the necessary forms. The petitioners must also take a written test. It checks their knowledge of English and of the history and government of the United States.

★ ★ ★ ★ ★ ★ ★ ★ ★ ★

Finally, the day of the court hearing arrives. This is the day that all new residents look forward to. In court, they promise to be loyal to the United States. Then the judge gives each person a certificate of citizenship. Congratulations resound throughout the courtroom. The new citizens can say with pride, "Today I am an American."

There was a special day like this in the lives of many of our parents, grandparents, neighbors, and friends. We need to learn what they had to do to become citizens of the United States. Then those of us who were born here can appreciate our citizenship even more.

★ ★ ★ ★ ★ ★ ★ ★ ★ ★

America is filled with people who came from other lands. All of us, except perhaps Native Americans, had family members who came here from another country. If we look back far enough in time, even the families of Native Americans came here from somewhere else—Asia.

How do we know this? Scientists think that thousands of years ago, a bridge of land connected Russia and Alaska. The families of Native Americans may have come to America across that land bridge.

Over the years, millions of people in countries all around the world have dreamed of settling in America. For many, coming here was very hard. For others, the trip was not only difficult, but also quite dangerous. Many people have been willing to risk their lives to come to America. Their dream is that one day, they would be able to say, "Today I am an American."

Why did so many people wish to come to America? Why do so many people around the world still wish to come here? A chance for a better job, a better life, and religious and political freedom attracted people from all over the world in the past. It still does today. Some who come here are trying to escape from a war in their home country. Others are escaping from a place where there are few jobs and little food.

Try to imagine your family suddenly packing up and moving to another country. All you can take with you is what you can pack into a couple of suitcases. If you are traveling with your family, at least you will have company. Still, the move will be difficult and scary.

When you get to the new country, you may not know how to read or speak the language there. Most likely, you have very little money. What will happen if it takes you a very long time to find a job? What will you do if your money runs out? Where will you live? How will you eat? Will you make new friends? Will anybody be willing to help you if you run into trouble? What if you can never see your parents, other relatives, or close friends again?

These are some of the many things people consider before deciding to come to America. Leaving behind a familiar world to go to a strange land takes a great deal of courage.

People view coming to America as a chance to enrich their lives. It is amazing that so many people have the courage to follow their dreams. America is happy to receive them because their talents, skills, and hard work enrich our country.

During the late 1800s and the early 1900s, a huge wave of people arrived in the United States. Between 1892 and 1920, about 23 million people from England landed in New York at Ellis Island. There they began the process of being admitted into the United States.

As the people walked off the ship, they were led into a building on Ellis Island. Inside, they had to answer questions and take a physical exam. Some people failed the physical. They were not allowed to remain in the United States. They soon found themselves on the next boat heading back to Europe.

You can imagine the confusion in the building where all these people's papers were processed. Many of the people could not speak English and could not understand the questions they were asked. The crowded hall must have resounded with anxious voices speaking many different languages. The officials would grow impatient. Often, they gave the people certificates with names that were totally different from their real names. Sometimes, in error, people were given the name of the town from which they had come!

Nobody apologized for rushing people through this process. Nobody apologized for giving them the wrong names. Because the people wanted to be accepted into the country, they were not about to complain.

Today many people still want to come to America to make a fresh start in life. They still need to apply for permission to stay in the United States. Many challenges face anyone who decides to come and live in the United States. Still, America keeps alive the hopes and dreams of millions all over the world. To be able to say "Today I am an American" is, for many, a dream come true.